MoneyMaking & The 1/3 Principle

Author: Garry Louis

MoneyMaking Guide 1st Edition

ISBN: 0615917186
ISBN-13: 978-0615917184

INTRODUCTION

Moneymaking has always been an idea for people to emancipate themselves and satisfy their desire to trade. They would travel many miles and cross the seas from one continent to another regardless the difficulties that they had to face form one point to another. They would never discourage because they would see it as a way to satisfy themselves and accumulate wealth.

They had done it with so much effort and passion from land to land to market their products even though they did not speak the same language. The idea of making money for them was to be at the rendez-vous and sold their merchandises. They would often leave without knowing their destination. They spent days and even months traveling with the hope to find a place to sell their products.

They were very well motivated to face the challenges that came their ways to reach their goals of selling their items and returned home with the satisfaction to support their families. During that market there was no distinction of color, race, and/or language. They would sell what they had and traded other items to return back home.

There was no technology involved. The market only needed a human mind to operate. None of them had to go to management school to complete the tasks. It was the old day. However, those days have gone. The concept of making money has become bigger over years. We are now having management schools and strategies to earn more money. The cost of living has changed and we have to earn more to support our families as compared to the previous era.

We have more structure in place and can beat any distance in less time than we used to. We have more needs, more orders, and more demands, which have us to explore the margin of expenses and profit. As a result we struggle to make money to avoid being in debt or bankrupt.

When most of us have looked into the opportunity to earn a paycheck in order to satisfy our needs, we come up short every month. Eventually the job market can only satisfy a few. Some companies are complaining about not making enough or any profit to satisfy employees' salaries. Some other companies are making a lot and keep them all for themselves.

We have tried to understand those changes around us because we have more obligations and more tasks to accomplish to support our families. We have developed more habits, routines, and have to learn newer skills to survive the changes.

For any reason that may seem to predetermine our way of living we have to fight to find a solution in order to be able to earn enough to respond to our needs. Nevertheless, with the realization of advanced technology, people have looked for resources online to earn a living; where they can easily find a place to fill out an application or an opportunity to work part time at home.

Many have revealed to be satisfied with their searches online using search engines like Google, Yahoo, Bing, and so on. Although they have been able to find something online, they are still concerned about not making enough to support their families. For that reason alone people are looking to make an extra income to respond to their family needs.

The MoneyMaking process is a new method designed to teach people new strategies to earn an extra income. The MoneyMaking Guide is on the market to help families finding the resources and teach them the basic to make money working fewer hours.

The MoneyMaking process is a simple method that describes a 1/3 principle to help individuals to earn a living and also to teach them how to invest to earn great returns at the end of the investment term. It is a proven method revealed to meet the needs of others expectations.

The MoneyMaking process is a drawing of data processing that requires no profound knowledge but discipline in other to process received and sending data within the expected window of time. It requires discipline to validate the resources and keep the records in place.

The MoneyMaking process offers a lot of advantages to the ones who share the interest in working a couple of hours processing data. The guide details the various ways people can make money and also describe the business structure for the ones who are looking forward to become entrepreneurs.

The MoneyMaking process guide provides a 1-2-3-step process for anyone to start generating data and making money without having to think about long term adaptation and ability to do well. The system is very easy to apply. You can use it as a new tool to make money while making plan to attend one of our trainings that include Real Estate Relocation, Stocks, and Media to strengthen your skills.

A model of the MoneyMaking process is provided with the NewAvenue, our company to help understand the structure and guide you through the process. All the necessary elements and forms are well described to help you understand the process.

Take the time to read the application. There is no fine print. Everything is clearly stated in black and white. The MoneyMaking process is an easy application designed to meet the needs of the people who are looking for something to do and earn an extra income. We offer three products that require people to subscribe.

Take the time to see if you can be a part of these promotions. Good Luck!

The realization of The MoneyMaking process guide vol. 1 is an accumulation of the knowledge and experiences in my field of study and practice. I would ever continue without mentioning my teachers and love ones who encourage me to reach my goals.

During my first year of my enrollment in English course, I attended D. A. Dorsey and Lindsey Hopkins. Then I continued at Miami Dade College taking college courses to pursue my goals at FAMU, USF, and Walden University.

My achievement today is to honor my mother, my father, my teachers, and fewer of my colleagues and managers that include Dr. James Simmons, Dr. Joseph Baldwin, Dr. Titus Brown, Dr. Allan Bellups, Dr. John Davis, Dr. Hebert Exum, Dr. Yolanda Bogan, Dr. Eric Toren, Dr. Ben Kinnard, Anna Lamazares, Loismet, Dr. Demco, Mike Verena, Robert Drake, Joseph Muller, Guercin Eduard Economist, Mike Filsaime, and so on.

CONTENTS

ACKNOWLEDGMENTS

The 1st. edition of the MonenyMaking & The 1/3 Principle describes the factors that impaired the economy and the difficulties that increase the likelihood for families to experience financial hardship.

The guide reveals the hidden secrets that many have used to take advantages of others. It describes several ways that people can adopt and earn an extra income. It also encourages them to become entrepreneurs in order to better structure and monitor their future plans.

MoneyMaking & The 1/3 Principle is a guide to help others comprehend the process of making money and build a wealth. The cover page for the 1st edition has a drawing of Dream Time collection from Google to help frame the content of the book.

1 MONEYMAKING

The job market has changed. The job requirements are more than what they used to be a decade ago. For one to be hired today, he/she has to meet all the specific requirements and convince the boss that he/she can do the miracle to contribute to the agency life profit. Otherwise, another substantial candidate will be next interviewed.

The job market has changed so much that the boss does not even want to pay the regular post salary. Employers prefer to hire a few people for the e job rather than hiring the number of people that could probably handle it.

Employers don't pay benefit anymore and the employees, unfortunately, have to hold their positions to be able to provide for their families and/or face their family situations.

10, 20 years ago, employers would do the hiring process with a guaranteed benefit packet that would offer everything ranking from a 401 K or B plan to a life insurance plan. Nevertheless, these set of benefits have long changed. The job position does not give any security or stability for families to plan their children futures. For instance, a head of household used to hold his/her job for many years and would retire with a good 20 or 30 years of pension. Consequently, today the employee is only hired for a 2-year contract without promotion.

Children of our generation cannot even get the job they apply for and when they do the hiring position does not offer any benefit or/and a reasonable salary. As a result, children of our generation have more debts with no hope to achieve their goals or meet their short-term expectations.

Having a job is the only thing that helps make our parents and brothers and friends who are not born from a wealthy family to feel proud having the certainty they can provide for their families and support themselves. Children of our generation have seen an increase in the unemployment rate that has affected their family lives and/or personal relationships. To partially balance the equation, I encourage you to check the resources that are now available to you.

During the last two decades, moneymaking process has been translated into a new language to motivate individuals and promote multiple ways to make money in the comfort of their homes.

Moneymaking is a process that can help you to free yourself by securing your future and living the life you always dream of. There are several ways that one can familiarize him/herself with the moneymaking process.

Having a great idea to become an entrepreneur such as by opening a small business, registering with a franchise corporation to earn supplement income, or working on your own to make a reasonable profit or residual income is obviously one of the significant ways to succeed in life. However, one of the best ways to make money nowadays has been proven to be working part time doing Data Entry or rebate processor Jobs online.

People who work part time from the comfort of their homes have revealed to make more money within a couple of hours and able to quit their jobs after a few weeks.

Moneymaking process is an idea. It is also a challenge that requires one to change his/her daily living routine by learning a 1-2-3 step process that will improve his/her knowledge or enhance his/her skills to earn money within hours working at home and be able to satisfy his/her desires, needs, and support his/her family.

There are many affiliate programs online that support the idea of moneymaking process. This is not always a scam. One has to believe in it and make the effort to research the appropriate sites that drive his/her curiosity and provide the basic knowledge for a good start in the Data Entry or processing rebates online.

Eventually, I am encouraging you today to customize yourself with the moneymaking process by having a small business or becoming an online affiliate that will give you the opportunity to work towards your future goals to succeed in life if you commit yourself to the program you choose.

You can choose to become an Amazon Affiliate, buy from us, or think about what you want to do. Our company offers a couple of opportunities to help you reach your goals. To learn more, visit our company links.

We are here to support ideas and offer quality services to you our customers and future affiliates. You can register with us to help your business grow or buy from us with confidence when shopping on our sites Www.MoneyMaking.com, Www.NewAvenue.US, Www.NewAvenue2020.com, Www.Eve77Stores.com

Our purpose is to sell you good ideas as well as quality products and encourage you to become an affiliate so you can formulate your own ideas and earn extra income to support your family. Fill free to visit our sites any time. You can register to join our projects, become one of our departmental allies, and use the available resources to get a fresh start. You can always leave us a comment on our sites. Www.facebook.com/garry.louis, Www.NewAvenue.US/Blog, Www.LinkedIn.com/Groups/DealerPros, Www.LinkedIn.com/Groups/Eve, and Www.Earth24.Me

We offer various ways to make money online. You can start with any of our products. We have a great selection divided into several categories that will match at least one of your interests. If you already have an idea but does not know how to pursue it, there is a search key tool located for you on the top right of the home page for your search query.

NewAvenue, LLC business services and product lines include sports and accessories, software for small businesses, online marketing for mortgage loans, shopping malls, travel, trading, insurance, and social networking. It shelters other websites that include Www.glgetloans.com, Www.NewAvenue2020.com, Www.moneymaking.com, and Www.Eve77Stores.com

The sites are to educate others about ways to make money working at home part time. They also offer available work at home programs to facilitate families to understand and improve their living situations. Making money is a process. It will never happen by staying home without doing an activity. The only one factor that generates making money is production. You have to produce in order to make money. You can pick your choice, which ironically means well come to the real world.

Even though we acknowledge that people make money: playing lotto, betting, and playing games online today, there are several other ways to make money and support your family without having to respond to a boss. You can work part time at home and earn six figures income. You can offer quality services to people in your community knowing what their needs are or what is missing there. You can bring something new to the environment that can represent a plus for the residents in that area, since they don't have to go somewhere else to get that particular service, which will facilitate the way for growth and open the door for other opportunities.

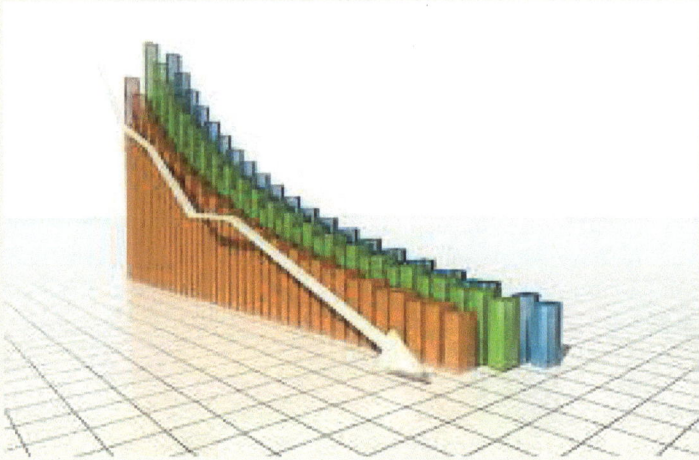

Fig. Job

This graph is chosen to give you a clear picture of the decline of the job market. The number of people unemployed is higher than the ones that have a job.

2 EMPLOYMENTS

If you do not have the opportunity to trade for now, which means not having any dispensable cash to take a forward step, you need to look for a job to earn and save a few bucks to structure your plans.

You may never nurture the idea to work or having a job; however a job is the key to your future because you have desires and dreams that you want to accomplish in your life. Having a job will give you the opportunity to identify yourself, to express your desires, and develop your plan. A job is an important element that you want to defy and specify since it will occupy most of your living time on earth.

You can choose to go to school to get a degree and operate on the basis of theory and knowledge skills. Many have decided not to be a scholar, buy to work on something they have routinely learned or worked doing something that is up to their abilities.

However, it will be always beneficial to you if you learn how to read and write to exercise your knowledge when you have an idea, rather than ask someone else to do everything for you.

You can prepare yourself to work in a field that you like, market yourself, work for companies, or better yet you can be self-employed working in your business. Whichever way you choose to go, you will need to make that choice for yourself because you have to

- Make money to survive
- Create a signature for yourself
- Support your family
- Achieve your goals, and
- Work on your future plans.

Doing something to make money is one of the major goals of everyone. For instance, during the teenage years most children nurture the idea to become an adult so that they can work to earn allowances and fulfill their desires. However, as adults we know that we have to work to face our responsibilities in life.

Making Money Online is one of the ultimate options today for many who have

chosen to service a distant population and market their products at a better rate.

You can work today a couple hours at home and earn a second income to support

your family. These resources are available to you now. To learn more you can buy

any of the selected eBooks that we are going to present to you in the following

pages or sites.

These tools are proven strategies and techniques with companies' connections to get you started without delay and make your decision according to the one that is most relevant to you.

Some people are interested in doing online surveys. This is one of the ways to make money. You don't have to have any specific skills or knowledge. A number of companies are looking to higher people for these particular tasks: online surveys, data entry, and so no. You only need to register and start making money.

They will pay you for your opinions once you agree to work with them. They will pay you for your efforts and the time you spent to complete the required tasks. It does not require much of time. You can do this simple work for two to three hours a day without having to deal with paper work deadlines and other requirements.

If you do have any other talents that you use every once in a while because you have been looking for other opportunities or ways to make money, you probably never think of it this way you can also make real money using your craft talent.

You can develop your talent to produce more and offer your own product to your customers. You can search the places that are looking to sell your products and ask them to inform you about their job application process. Look for the resources online to learn about the steps to help you start your business. You can make a difference doing what you do best.

Don't waist all your time looking for other things to do when you can use your own talent to move forward. To learn more we will provide you a few common links in the following pages to guide you through.

If you rather work in a workplace than do your own business, seek the resources to create your resume to very well market yourself so that your application can be withdrawn among the ones selected for the interview.

There are tools that are designed to help you prepare a professional resume when you market yourself out there in the field that you like. They provide strategies to help you personalize your resume to reflect exactly the position you are applying for.

You sometimes wander why they do not call you after you applied three times for the same position or submitted your application to more than three places. The key is you have to always look professional and see yourself as
- The only candidate for the job.
- Present your related skills or knowledge
- Your year experiences and/or training
- If no experiences, your internship is your ground
- Do a cover letter for your resume
- Get letter of recommendations from your teachers or coworkers

If you are recently looking for jobs or market yourself and do not know how to shape your future, you can always seek for resources online to help improve your skills and edit the areas of your resume accordingly. Believe in yourself and increase your confidence when you are going to attend your interview. When you market yourself, think of yourself as a good product. They will pick you because you have related skills and knowledge to convince them you are the one for the position.

The concept of moneymaking is for everyone to benefit from. It does not discriminate against skills, ability, knowledge, culture, ethnicity, race, religion, belief, or gender. That is the reason we develop the MoneyMaking process method to provide strategies that anyone can benefit from to earn an extra income to support their family.

If you are a single mother and struggling to find something to do to support your family, these tools also provide resources for you, Single moms can work part time at home or filing part time position online. These are great opportunities to help them support their families and respond to their children school requirements.

If you did not know to look for resources online nor had any fears thinking about what to do to support or raise your children, you can work part time at home today without worries or being stressed out. These resources can give you the satisfaction you have been looking for an opportunity to spend more time with your family.

Several years ago, people, families did not have the opportunity to look for job elsewhere. They had to commute within distances and had a contact person to get a job. However, in our modern age or the computer age where electronics devices are very advanced and updated you can easily train yourself, make plan, work toward your goals and earn more money working part time at home. Some of us have turned in to hobbies because they have a passion for what they like to do. There are many ways to go by the moneymaking process. There are several moneymaking guides that are written to help you through the process of making a decision to change your lifestyle and improve your situation.

If you do have a hobby that drives your passion, you spend much time doing it and never have time for anything else. It preoccupies you all the time. You have been doing it routinely for fun and only think about it. Eventually, you have news today. Your hobby can also help making you money. All you have to do is an online search query to look for available resources related to your interest.

For instance, David rides his bike to go to school rather than taking the bus. He plays basketball for his high school. However, he mentions that he likes to take pictures as a habit wherever he goes. He does a description of them and attaches them on his bedroom wall. Besides his school and the basketball team requirements he always makes time to shoot sceneries that he likes. David was suggested to create an online gallery to share his interest, connect with others, and explore what the outcomes would be by the time he graduates from high school. This simple chart is to give you an idea how David will connect with others within his online gallery.

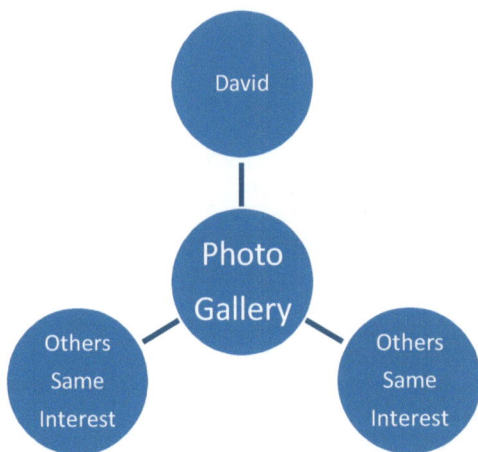

Many of us nurture the idea to becoming an entrepreneur or having a business. You do not need to know math or having any college skills to do this. But if you still would like to learn the basic skills or you are looking for one thing to do in that same manner, you can check related resources that provide strategies and techniques to help you through. Also further we will provide our company links with the specific details to help you with your choice.

Www.NewAvenue.US, Www.MoneyMaking.com, http://Www.earth24.me ,

Www.NewAvenue2020.com

3 BUSINESSES

Becoming an entrepreneur, having a business, or doing some type of activity that put you on the row as a self-employed are the healthiest ways to make a living. Imagine for a second that you are doing something to help others or satisfy the needs of your community that gives you in return peace of mind and not having to deal with someone else that pushes you around or call the boss. You are the author of your own self because you are the only one that develops and implements your daily plans.

When you are working to satisfy your boss you only fulfill the boss's desires. Consequently after long day of working hours you get more tired, unsatisfied, living pay check to pay check as they say, and could never reach your goals or support your family the way you suppose to.

In some instances, you produce more every day for less money. On the percentage you barely receive a dime of the third quarter from a quarter. I think you quickly realized how far you get to make it to a quarter while your boss is making (100 % of the production and sometimes 200 % of the production) all of it, pressured you, and stressing you out.

To illustrate making a plan to having a business is one of the most reputable processes in the making money history.

Have you had the idea to having a business before, ever thought about it, or you recently have the idea to having your own business or become an entrepreneur? If you are not there yet, it does not matter. You have time to plan your future and decide which of your goals you want to pursue.

Many of us like the idea to open a small business but never get to accomplish our goals. What's the inconvenient? Maybe we don't have the motivation to do it or we don't know how to get there. If this is your case, you probably want to talk to someone that can help you find resources or find something that you like to do and ask for advice. If you are on that corner, we encourage you to buy business eBooks from our sites, eBay, amazons, and/or sign up with Clickbank to help you structure your plans and make a decision that you can benefit from.

EBay Business
eBay is one of the most common market place and Internet Marketing online. EBay gives several options to buyers and sellers to open a store online with the idea to sell or buy something online. You can start by creating your eBay personal page and sell anything from your house online.

There are several ways you can sell an item on eBay. EBay has auction, wholesale, and buy it now process that satisfy the market process for both parties.

It's easy to register to buy and/or sell on eBay. Check the www.ebay.com site and follow the guidelines. We also offer integrated eBay market eBooks that can help you with the process of doing business on eBay.

These tools will teach you the techniques and strategies to buy from eBay, to sell, and make profit from the eBay market online. In addition you can register with a wholesaler to facilitate your way to eBay. You can learn the program and sell your product or a product of your choice online.

Having a business is a legitimate way to create a signature for yourself. It gives a unique impression to your friends, family, society you are a part of, and even expose your performance to the world you live in. It is fairly your contribution to the society. However, not everyone wants to have a business due to the inconveniences that associate with it.

Building a good relationship for your business is an outstanding element. Business owners have to use positive strategies to give quality services to customers so that they can improve the business and meet the demand of their customers.

You want to keep a virtual eye on your business to prevent irregularities from occurring. Often time businesses that are not structured disappeared on the map after three years. It is so hard to realize that after you got so far on the road, the road was an impasse and you had to go back to find your way. Eventually, as a business owner you need to be informed of the development of the business or learn the structure yourself to be able to rescue your business from upcoming difficulties.

Business owners have to learn to keep a book for the business to avoid overdrawn transactions that may impair the life of the business as it pertains to the business asset verses profit; which might be an indication of the reasons that few business owners lost their businesses every year. Many of them do not think it is necessary to keep an eye on the expenses once they have good transactions. They quickly feel comfortable and believe that things have changed for good.

However, all the reviewed statistics have proved otherwise. Most businesses did not survive after a couple of years due to a lot of factors that concerned the business owners and poor data application.

The application of the data requires discipline and knowledge not routine to be able to maintain the files and satisfy the coordination within internal and external departments selected to process the data and work toward the achievement of the company success. In the following chapters we will defy data processing.

The business existence is strongly relied on the product quality and the customers' demands. Due to that fact business owners have to market their businesses products to reach out more targeted customers and meet the demands. The marketing will help to announce the business product, meet the community needs, and increase the business transactions.

Having a business is to offer a service and/or product that meet the requirement to satisfy the need of a community that might be local or international. See how the business operates

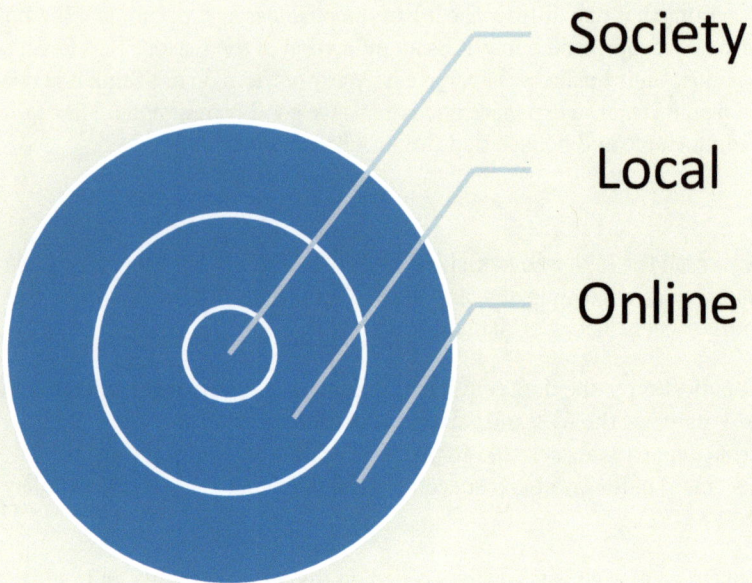

4 MARKETING

Marketing itself is a very broad concept and idea. There are several ways to market your business and/or products. Business owners have their own tendencies toward marketing. Some owners adopt them all. But some of them only consider a particular choice to announce their business. Marketing involved many form of advertisements or announcements that include:

- Local flyers

- Ads

- Presentations

- e-mail

- Media

- Event

Business owners use local flyers as an option to publicize their businesses in their relative communities. Local flyer is a very simple application and effective way to reach out targeted customers. It requires fewer expenses and offers the opportunity for clients to locate the resource rather than doing a search.

Some businesses use Ads through Advertisements site like Google, Amazon, Yahoo, Bing, and/or on the social media pages to increase their impression and sales. This application costs more than the local flyer but gives more positive results in returns. Most businesses use it because they can reach a greater number of customers and sell their products locally and online.

Presentation is a form of marketing that requires business owners or agents that represent the company to persuade others to listen to the company definition and buy the company products. A lot of businesses use that application to recruit and reach out potential customers because it gives them the opportunity to defy, market the products, describe the needs, and seek common interests.

Companies send emails to communicate with employees, members, and customers. However, sending bulk of emails has also become a practice to reach customers and market their products. This application does not require much to do. Everyone can do it in the comfort of his or her home. It only requires to having an available list.

Media is what would probably consider now as the master plan to move up a business to the next level. Media involved more than 300 channels that include advertise on radio, TV, the social pages such as Facebook, Twitter, LinkedIn, Classifieds Ads, Reddit, Add This, and so on. The application of the media demands précised data processing management to provide effective results.

The use of media is simple and accurate. It requires to having basic knowledge of advertisement to place ads and connect them together for effective results. The media channels are great in numbers and offer the flexibility to market your product to the world in several languages.

Event is a form of open marketing that companies or organizations use to market their products and capture the Aim from the fans. It is a great application for companies to use because the fans are excited to invest on the product and cannot wait to see the manifestation of it. This type of advertisement offers a broader console for effective results.

Blogging is one of the common application tools that individuals, businesses, and professionals used today to share their idea, experiences, and market their products. If you have not yet done it or do not know how to do it we provide a model and links for you to learn from.

Although advertisements offer great hope to the future of a business some businesses still do not advertise due to the lack of knowledge of the business owners and the various costs of media orders. We expect that our guide provides the direction you intended to follow to structure your business.

Our special links are:

Www.NewAvenue.US

Www.NewAvenue2020.com

Www.NewAvenueLLC.com

http://www.earth24.me

5 BLOGGING

If you are looking for a shorter way rather than having a business for now, blogging is the modern way of making money. It has become very common recently and many of us have turned to it to earn a living. Not everyone likes to write or takes time to read about a subject, but reading remains the best ways to seek information or available resources at first hand.

I am a member of a few elite groups (Auto Power Blogs, Blogger, & Wordpress) that helps and teaches people the strategies to blog and sell on line. If you get to that portion of my text I encourage you to check my links in order to have a constructive idea about the resources that are available to you.

You can blog your ideas on a subject matter or something you develop an interest for to make money. You can also blog articles, your comments or testimonials on services that please you and make money. Blogging is one of the fastest profit machines that can help you to implement your ideas and share your interest with others.

If you have ever done so you need to start today. Pick any subject or topic that you feel comfortable to talk about and do it at your own pace. You can use simple strategies to get your flow going.

Brainstorming for instance is a writing element that can help you gather your thoughts and produce more ideas as you go along with that adventure. It's in your head. Type or write on a piece of paper all the words that are relevant to you or better explain the relevance of your subject and categorize them in three segments or groups.

These three segments will help you to structure and complete three simple paragraphs that explain your ideas. One of the best strategies that work all the time you can ask questions??? To guide others through your thoughts.

Other than brainstorming you can create a list of "How to and Ws" to associate your ideas and help the reader to understand your point.

- What that identifies a specific event
- Why that explains the reason or cause
- Where that indicates the location and describes the scene
- Who that represents individual, people, company, or entity involved
- When that specifies the time and possibly the duration
- How that explains the frequency and sequences

Blogging is a simple way to express yourself, share your ideas, experiences, and/or knowledge on a subject matter with others. It helps you to gather your ideas and implement your skills. It does not put any pressure on you to complete related tasks. You can choose to save the draft and add another segment to it, or publish it. If you have ever done so, start whenever you like. In every practice, there is always a first time. Be ready to start and apply the tools that are available to you to enhance your knowledge.

Eventually, in a long run it will no longer be a matter for you. You will be able to explain your thoughts and develop your own style. Many don't like to write because they feel that they do not know much about the subject. However, if you blog you can be as simple or quick as you like and go right to the point.

To expand your ideas and illustrate your topic, you can also use a professional list that includes:

- The goal The purpose
- The mission
- The plan
- The problem targeted
- The inconveniences or barriers
- An alternative
- The solution

Or you can choose all of the above and emphasize on the necessary points that you want to discuss or talk about. Do it at your own pace. You can blog for fun, to share, to express, to develop an interest in a particular area, or simply to comment on someone else's topic.

Open yourself to explore the flow coming out of you that will inspire you to write more and contribute in some way to the blogging world that may motivate, educate, or open the way to others in building agendas.

Now for the presentation or the look of your final work, one of my teachers recommended that you write short paragraphs and leave two spaces between them. When you do so your presentation easily catches the readers' attention, for they can easily read and understand your ideas. To remember for your illustration, a good story helps the reader to focus more.

Now you are ready to blog get one of the tools offered to guide you through and improve your skills. To learn more about blogging here are a few suggested links:

Www.NewAvenue.US, Www.MoneyMaking.com

Www.earth24.me

Although marketing is a very broad knowledge, many choose to do it to earn a living. Besides blogging, to many young people the idea of making money is to record a CD. They are really passionate about it and want to make it happen because they often see it as the only way to emerge.

When I went to college years ago, almost every young man nurtured that same idea to be an R&B singer or a Rapper to make money. They would very often created their CDs and sell them after classes. However, most of them did not succeed due to a lot of factors.

- The 1990s were the new era for computers and electronic devices.
- People have pagers
- Computers and cell phones were very expensive and not every student could afford them.
- IPod and music download were not there yet as a privilege
- Pitch tone devices were expensive and were not easy to find
- To make a good song a band and a studio were necessary
- And you know the rest most of them would not make the cut if you have well hears for music.

However, nowadays, all of these have changed. You can easily learn how to read music notes, play an instrument, or improve your pitch. You simply have to learn the strategies and practice to get effective results. Many of us have talents but we somehow are too busy and don't take time to develop our skills or increase our ability to perform well.

You can do it and be good at it, motivate yourself and make the efforts to reach that goal, either to sing, to improve your talent, enhance your pitch, or market your music. Whichever decision you make to achieve your goals will take you closer to the realization of your dream ideas and earn more money as you grow in your professional field.

The electronic devices are available and affordable. You can buy eBooks, video lessons, and related software that only focus on your interests. You can do music yourself, do it to help others, and market your skills or talents as you go along and make more money.

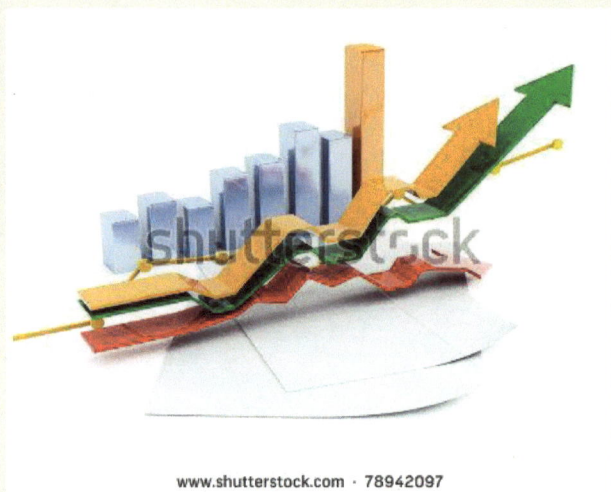

www.shutterstock.com · 78942097

6 INVESTMENTS

Although an investment may reflect in many ways the formation of a business, investment as a practice has not been yet completely understood to be a focus for many of us. It includes ways, discipline, some basic knowledge, and cash requirements.

Most of us would like to invest sometime in our lives; however, we do not know where and how to proceed with that particular goal. Because we all would like to have security in our lives to support family, and ourselves we look into buying a house and having a vehicular engine to commute from one location to another and meet our jobs criteria.

We always think that we need a capital to invest or we need to go to the bank to start. As far we look into it most investment agreements would determine an initial amount and terms. In reality one cannot benefit from it because one does not have the knowledge of what he/she is doing.

Investment is one of the best decisions you can make for yourself or your family.

Although there are several ways to invest your money, the NewAvenue, our company provides for you three particular ways to choose from and make a decision.

- <u>Stocks</u>
- Real Estate
- Green Energy

Stocks

Investment is one of the best decisions you can make for yourself or your family. Although there are several ways to invest your money, it requires some thought to make sure that you are taking a step for the future. An investment does not give quick results after a couple of months or so. It takes time and more time relating to the type of investment you engage in.

If you choose to buy stocks, for instance, you have to allow some time to see results. It is not to see significant growth after a year if you are looking to earn quick cash.

How do you like to invest your money or how much do you know about stocks and bonds? Are these words sound familiar to you or maybe you think you could never be a part of it due to financial hardship or family situation. Different types of stocks and education are designed to help individuals who are looking to invest in stocks or share common interest for stocks.

There are a variety of eBooks written on stocks that will give you the basic knowledge of trade and help you understand the evolution of the stock market. Most of us who do not know the culture of the stock market do not want to engage in or spend the time to learn about it. However, stockbrokers and stock investors are very passionate about it and would not go through the day without checking the stock news. We would like to encourage you to read about it. To learn more about buying stocks or getting a membership you can visit the investment links on our site

After you get a membership from my site if you are still confused and would like to work with a broker to guide you through your membership process, I recommend you to go to etrade.com and/or Zecco.com

Real Estate/Buying a House

Do you have in mind to buy a house? Or are you planning to buy a house? Whichever thought nurtures your objectives will guide you through if you have a good plan or are looking for the resources to implement it. If you do not know about the steps to take, start now seeking the resources to make an educated decision.

Some people don't buy a house only because they think they don't have money to buy a house or belief they are not making enough to make a decision like this. Some others are just not ready due to being in debts.

If you are in debts you need to think about a way to repair your credit. That situation alone can drag you down and offer the opportunity to others to keep you down. When you don't get out there these things will hold your future.

- Collection debts agencies are making money of you and will not let you live in peace with harassing phone calls.

- The rate for your credit card will be higher than everybody else.

- If you are renting, your deposit and rent will be higher than the standard

- You need to know that if you are living with a relative, roommate, or renting an apartment, you are spending a lot of money to satisfy someone else projects.

Buying a home will give you the privilege to become a homeowner and maximize your opportunity to live your dream. You will live with the confidence knowing that this is your place and whatever you do to it will be at your calculated risk.

Despite all the saying and fear people share about buying a home, it is always better for someone to take that first step and in a long run that person will be glad that he/she did. The truth is that when you are renting, the money you are spending will never come back to you or you will never benefit from it.

Now is the right time for you to make a decision that will benefit you in every way possible. We encourage you to think about it if you feel that you are not in condition to make a step like this. Buying required to having the opportunity to trade. What we mean by that you enter a store you give money for an item based on the price tag and the item is delivered to you.

In the US and few other Countries you can buy house cash or on terms, which means that you can get a mortgage loan based on the qualification requirements such as having a job and so on to buy a house for 15 or 30 years.

With that logic in mind we want to say that you can buy:

- Based on the price tag
- Based on your possibility
- Get the one that fits your budget

Buying a house is a serious commitment that you choose to make for yourself or/and your family. Be smart and make the right choice. Prepare yourself to live the moment you always dream of. Remember everything starts with an idea. Think about it and make it happen. Stop listening to the ones who say you cannot do it.

There are many reasons that prompt us to motivate you to buy a house or think about it to the best of your possibilities.

- The competition in real estate is not always a priority
- Mortgage rates are very low
- There are more foreclosure home in the market every day
- The opportunity for first home buyer is greater than before

Now if you have landed on that page and read that far you have made the first step to help you fix your situation or make the decision to buy your house. We provide resources for you that give you options to buy, sell, or making an investment as you desire.

On this page you will find the links and sites info that will help you move along with your ideas, your projects, and reach your goals. Remember buying a house is the first step to accumulate wealth and provide a shelter for your family. This means that you can use the house to pursue other plans and realize your dreams.

After the market crashed a few years ago the competition in real estate has experienced a decline in proportion that affected entrepreneurs, realtors, developers, and homeowners. The buyer has more options where the seller has fewer choices. Most mortgage brokers withdrawn from the market leaving the banks in control with more criteria to buy.

No one ever expected to witness such variation in the real estate market. Mortgage rate was between 2.5-4.6 for the first time. Although sellers could afford to buy a house cheaper, the market was still down due to there were fewer buyers and sellers could not make any prediction on the sales.

More foreclosure homes every day in the bank folders increased the inventory and stopped the market from moving forward. Many homeowners got out of their deed commit with the banks to survive on a short sale receipt that did not offer any advantages or future hopes.

The opportunity has become greater for the buyer; however only a few could benefit from it because the economy crisis that left most families without a job or enough saving to fulfill the American dream of buying a home. Some others were indebted and did not have any way out.

With that situation have emerged a lot of companies that offer services for a modification program either to scam or to resolve that matter. The ones who could understand and experience the drastic changes of the market feared to invest or to take part.

Shortly after we designed a moneymaking system to encourage others to invest and benefit from the market. The moneymaking process idea always works because the Revenue on Investment (ROI) is proportional to change. We will explain this in further chapters. There is only one consideration for result: the demand. To learn more or find appropriate services check these links.

Www.glgetloans.com

Www.NewAvenue.US

Www.MoneyMaking.com

http://Www.earth24.me

The Inconveniences After Buying a Home

The inconveniences after buying a home are taxes, taking a second lean as a result of being in debts, and foreclosure as a result of default payments on the property. However, knowing how to deal with taxes and staying out of debts can help the house owner in both ways that might include saving and making money.

When you finally bought your home remember you have to stay vigilant and be aware of the conveniences that may affect your home or your investment.

Property taxes are one of the common issues that sometimes arise and impair homeowners' abilities to keep their assets, which imperatively lead to foreclosure and/or get them to lose their homes.

Property Tax

Be aware of the factors associated with property taxes will prevent you from going into a lot of difficulties. Being behind on your payments due to lack of support or not knowing the proper procedures to follow may cause you to lose your home. We discuss about several options for you. We would like to help you or you can search the resources on our sites and learn how to do it.

We provide answers and resources for tax questions that involved your residential and commercial property taxes. At the bottom of the page, check the links and find the ones that most relevant to you.

Buying Commercial & Residential Properties/Taxes

It is not always difficult to find commercial and residential properties to buy or sell. Individuals have developed an interest for these types of investment. Over the years it has become very popular and a growing market for entrepreneurs and others who want to buy into the market or explore it.

However it requires time to understand the market and be able to adapt to the concepts of tax reductions for properties. Some people believe that they can only invest and make money form it while they are trying to escape the financial education about properties and relevant taxes.

When you invest in residential and commercial Real Estate it requires a level of understanding of tax appeal and tax reduction process to effectively gear your success. When you reach that confidence level you can fill out paper work and proceed on follow up taxes without any difficulties.

Although there are a lot of differences between residential and commercial investments as well as the way the taxes are processed, it is important to gather the factors that can help you handle your taxes effectively.

For instance, if you bought a house a few years ago, you were instructed to have a separate company to handle your taxes. Sometimes they give you the options to pay quarterly or annually based on other criteria that may well relate to the process. If by any means you forgot or failed to pay taxes on your property while paying your mortgages you may incur a balance that you have to pay back to the state to prevent you from losing your house.

The difference between residential and commercial taxes is that taxes are higher for commercial properties due to the fact that you have the ability to make profit on them. In addition commercial property owners do not usually handle taxes themselves since they often have business manger or accountant to complete that process. However, if that does occur, they still have to pay back taxes or follow the tax appeal process according to regulations that may in any way affect the business.

Tax lien is one of them. For these reasons it is important to cover the tax provisions at the time of the purchase to avoid those irregularities, extend the life of your investment, and handle your taxes with care.

To learn more about residential and commercial taxes, protect your investment, and increase your margin for profit, we provide resources for you.

Foreclosure
As we have been anticipated, Foreclosure has been one of the Echo News for the past several years. Nobody ever expected or knew that the downfall of the market would hit on Real Estate that way. Investors have lost their businesses and families have lost their homes.

What causes all that?

The fact is that families have debts and have lost their jobs. They could no longer support themselves and their love-ones In addition to that we have

- The cost of living,

- Mortgage rate,

- Land pricing and value,

- High market tag value

They are associated factors that explain the fall. This issue has become a State concern that turns families to mortgage modification. But you still cannot save your house because you frankly do not know what to do, whom to talk to, and/or where to go.

They are associated factors that explain the fall. This issue has become a State concern that turns families to mortgage modification. But you still cannot save your house because you frankly do not know what to do, whom to talk to, or where to go. Visit our sites and explore our resources.

Foreclosure programs have been more common than before to prevent you from losing your home. They teach you the defense secrets of foreclosure, helps keep your home, and increases your confidence level.

The cost of living is very high nowadays and does not offer any option for the ones living paycheck to paycheck under a constant hope to create a better future for their children. Families have to keep working and meet the expectation cycle every month. On the contrary the magic number that maintains the main elements for change has ever been affected. It's the variance for demographic locations and the distance fuel that pitch the high.

When I graduated from college a few years ago I was told there was a standard salary for every profession relatively to knowledge and year of experiences. In most cases the standard was never respected. The production is high while the earning for the labor is very low with no margin for saving.

If you were to review the table for low Income families the cost of living would be about 3.7 higher than the earning cycle per month or per year. As it appear to be similarly strange and disturbing when you are renting they would mostly charge you more and even keep your return without any discussion or shame.

When you are renting they charge you more at the beginning. They tend to increase your lease during the contract or if you decide to continue. The likelihood is that in most cases they do not pay their property taxes; which clearly is an indication of poor management.

During a housing discussion we raised this issue: what to do when they keep your deposit without any reason? A friend of mine proposed that the tenant put it writing he/she will use the deposit at the end of the contract. Now remember if you keep that shelter like yours there is no legitimate reason for the landlord or the office management to keep your deposit.

Doing business does not mean giving the power to hackers, getting rich quick, offending people, and providing poor services. Regardless the nature of the business we need to provide quality services to customers.

Although buying a home is a great feeling, be aware of that mortgage brokers tend to incline on the insatiable taste of the ratio, which might affect the buyer's commitment toward the loaner. For instance we probably would have too much to say after the collapse of the real estate market a few years ago.

It is obvious that many of us understand that the price tag escalated too fast in most regions to satisfy a market that did not have a stable future. Where's the balance? Here is the reason to having the desire to earn an extra Income.

Learning the process how to make money working part time has become an essential idea for many of us. The moneymaking process is one of the leading methods reveal to help you identify the factors and earn an extra income.

Why Green Energy?

Green energy is a new approach that uses solar panel and wind power to transform electrical energy. Research has proven that this type of energy will produce more power in a short time with less combustion.

According to the sources and news, solar energy is proven to be highly profitable to consumers because it reduces their electric bills from 50-75% every month. They speculate that residents will have the choice to both get solar and wind power or ordinary electricity in their home.

Solar energy is a new market and it is speculated to make entrepreneurs great profits in the future, Many people do not know yet about solar energy but they only feel that in some times they will have to find a solution to reduce the course of energy that may include electrical power, engine combustion, and possibly the correction for the rising of air pollution in the cities.

Home Energy
It is good to feel comfortable at home when you can use your power energy for your needs without thinking too much about how high the utility bills will be for the month.

During the hot weather we use the air conditioning more than we use to in the intent to maintain our body temperature and not feeling sweaty. During the cold weather, on the other hand, we use the hit to stay warm in order to condition ourselves and continue doing our activities.

Either way we cannot stop thinking about the utility bills. We always have to make adjustment due to the changing weather or to satisfy our needs.

Besides we cook and eat a lot. We entertain at home watching TV, listening to music, or playing computer games, and so on.

We do not want to deal with the utility bill because it damages our wallet, but it would not be fair either to forget how we use the service. There is maybe a better way to continue dealing with the stress we put on ourselves while we commit to our activities and make adjustment to the changing weather.

We think that a new approach to use power for your home is more efficient, which will give you another way to save your money.

Using solar power energy is a proven system that fewer people have been turned to as another choice or alternative to reduce their electricity bills up to 50 or 75%.

Does this sound too good to be true to you or you want to give it a try? There are more than one options to do this you can try it yourself with the knowledge we are going to provide you or we can get one of the best companies to do the installment for you. Whichever way you chose to do it you will be happier. Now check our resource and get the one you like better.

DiY Energy/Solar Panel

To learn more we offer a variety of resources that you can choose from. As we stated previously its major advantages include: reducing monthly electric bills, increase DiY energy, and reducing pollution in the Cities using gas electric car conversions and battery reconditioning for cars and green business.

To be in business or an entrepreneur it is more profitable to you to have some basic knowledge in order to be able to read basic notes that attach your business to some other files. Being able to read is a gift that will increase your ability reach your goals in that manner.

Having a handicap or not having the ability to do so we suggest that you hire someone to manage those data. In the moneymaking process this step will inform you about the condition of your business networking.

When we talking about investment you can choose to buy green business products or invest directly with the companies that are out there offering this particular service. They can install your solar panel at a discount price; do your car electric conversion, and more.

Our Company, the NewAvenue does not offer green business services, but we promote that type of investment and can assist you as requested.

The following figures are to explain the different types of investment in stocks and Real Estate.

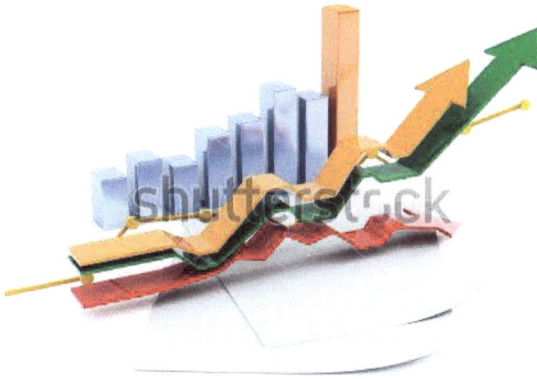

www.shutterstock.com · 78942097

If you were to invest in an aggressive stocks and expected to have a return of 12% - 17% at the end of the investment term that might be 5, 7, or 10 years, your stock investment would energetically increase to reach your expectation. However, when the market is down it would only affect your return.

The first arrow indicates how well the stock is working. The second one indicates the fluctuation of the market. The red arrow shows the fall or the standard level of the market.

This figure clearly explains the rise and fall of the market.

If you were to invest in Real Estate as an entrepreneur you would buy on the property value or tag price. Your investment would base on ROI Revenue on Investment rather than a significant ratio.

Entrepreneurs invest in Real Estate to create cash flow or earn great return on investment. If a house is bought for $50,000.00 and sold for 80,000.00 the entrepreneur made a profit for $30,000.00 on that investment.

The banks adopt a formula to sell for 15 or 30 year through mortgage transaction with a fix or conventional interest rate. When the bank sold a property the bank made a profit about 2 ½ times of the price value.

The buyer who wants to buy for 15 or 30-year term with a fix rate will pay the same interest rate for the term of the mortgage.

The investment figure shows the bank's profit:

When the bank invested on a property, the band will always have a great return regardless the condition of the market. The bank only lost when the number of bank's own property is higher than the bank's investment assets on property and directly proportional to the fall of the market.

Debt Factors

Your credit score is down. You don't know what to do to improve it. You probably enrolled in several programs in the past and still have the same problem. You are thinking and looking for a solution. You have not found a way out yet.

Some say if you pay them in full you would be better. Have you tried that as a solution? You paid them all and keep them in your wallet. Others say close all of them. Haven't you tried that either?

When you paid them all it does not work because you used them again. When you close them all it does not work either because you have to buy things that do not accept cash.

What to do then??? We have a solution for you. We suggest that you take a look at the NewAvenue plan our company that we will present to you in the next following chapters, or visit our site and improve your situation.

There are several Credit Repair programs to fix your credit. They are proven to be effective and easy method to fix and improve your credit score. Some of them will train you about the five effective ways to repair your credit.

Have you been in debt for years, owe $10.000 or more, and you do not know what to do?? Or you filed for bankruptcy because it was your way out. You have a car and a family. You are paying rent or having a mortgage. You are not making enough to pay your debts and still have to be there for your love ones.

Your life has been different since then. You cannot buy anything or fulfill your desire. You are in the midst of everything but cannot reach your goals. You want to get out of debts and continue working on your plan for your life.
Have you ever checked your credit score to find out where you at on that chart? Are you aware of your situation? Or you are afraid to check it because you spent too much and do not want to know.

Maybe you are in crisis, having financial difficulties; you do not know what to do. It is very important to be aware of your situation, so that you know what to do to move forward. You need to regain your confidence and resolve your problem.

We want to help you get there. These programs are proven evidence that can completely remove all traces of errors, facts, and false endorsements that are considered to be very sensitive information in your credit report. Please take the time to read and adopt the one that can help you to improve your credit score, your future, and as well protect your identity, your job, your investment, and your relationship.

 In the near future NewAvenue will open his door to help the ones that are in needs. We offer different products to help repair your credit, but read carefully and buy the one that is most suited to your situation.

You are probably very discouraged by now due to not being able to find a solution after enrolling in a few lousy programs. You still have a chance. You are not the only one to experience that situation. You can still fix it. If you had done so in the past, keep doing it until you resolve that matter. Our team will be more than welcome to assist you.

Some of the Guides are effective proven credit repair methods to increase your credit score in 90 days. Some of them are well-known methods to remove chapter 7 and chapter 13 bankruptcies from your credit report.

Be aware of the inconveniences that might come your way. As compared to living cost and standard salary, your credit score is well maintained and very calculated. Folks would do you the favor to match the numbers for you even after sunset.

In addition, your credit score or financial status cannot completely impair your ability to reach your dreams. If you have an idea you can motivate yourself and choose one of the resources that are out there to earn an extra income and start working on your goals.

In fact to get out of debts you need money to pay the fees. Therefore there are a thousand ways to do this. You can create, find, or sell a product to make money. You can also choose the MoneyMaking process to earn an extra income generating data.

To start you need to register, fill out the form and follow the procedures. There is no contract and no fine print. Every statement is clear and well defined. Please, take the time to read the document.

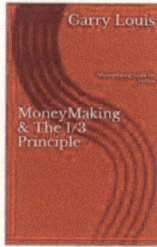

7 READING VS TECHNOLOGY

Most of us struggle to adapt to the learning process of reading and writing even in our native language because it requires time and efforts to understand the verb and discern logical reasoning from irrational thoughts. Although reading course is not considered to be high-level Science courses, it is imperative for everyone to learn how to read.

Having the ability to read indicates that the individual has an average IQ that makes him/her eligible to take science courses and have the ability to do science. The new generation is having difficulty to understand and complete training courses just simply they are not doing well in reading course.

Reading is also used as an open market to make money or a specified domain such as some people use reading claiming to predict others' future.

To illustrate, reading secrets is not geared toward reading skills or neither a complete element of health. It is more prone to reveal the inner side or the unconsciousness from the psyche. However, individuals who seek to understand occurrence events beyond reality and the power of human mind develop a passion for this study area. In the process of making money people use reading in several domains.

Getting control of your business is a fundamental process. Whichever way you may look at it, you revenue on investment (ROI) has to be one of the major concerns.

Some business owners value communication a lot and believe that it is important to learn a second language to multiply their customers.

Do you like to travel, meet people from other race, and develop the interest to learn a new language? A second language is a Q that identifies our milieu, interest, ethnicity, country, culture, habits, values, and parts of our beliefs system. The ones that speak a second language have the ability to understand and expand the market for their products.

Indeed no one ever try to speak a language because they want to. It certainly reveals a sign of overcoming struggles if one is not of origin from that pole of the globe.

It might appear to be a barrier for the ones who have to learn a second language. For business owners or entrepreneurs regardless their immigrant status, it is important to interact and/or communicate with allied partners and customers in other countries.

Language is also an element that helps to advertise the business and market products. Some entrepreneurs accept that fact and develop an interest to learn a second language or team up with a foreigner to expand their businesses' connection and sells.

If for one reason or another you feel the need to speak a foreign language visit our special links. If you want to learn how to get more control in your business learning how to operate a computer will bring everything to you. You can work on your screen anywhere at any time with no restriction.

Our special links:
Www.NewAvenue.US
Www.NewAvenue2020.com
http://www.earth24.me
Www.MoneyMaling.com

Technology

History of Computers

Hundred years ago the evolution of technology appeared to be done gradually with special tasks in field of study that were maintained for their specific applications according to the flexibility of their used. For instance, in health and business, it is obvious that changes used to be seen in long term as comparing to results of outcomes that required more studies or reviews.

However with the rapid apparition of computers, technology has had suddenly challenged every field of study and increased their cell of expectations for better results. The outcome of that advance technology has influenced everything that counts for a living. Therefore, mega computers, personal and microcomputers today form the core history of computers and shape reality differently.

At one time mega computers were frequently used to relate data information about interior and exterior activities of countries. They were giants and were able to save and process a lot of information. For example, according to the book of Larry and Nancy Long on computers, "the ENIAC, first all electronic general-purpose digital computer, could perform calculations 1,000 times faster than its electromechanical predecessors.

It weighed 30 tons and occupied 1,500 square feet of floor space." J. Presper Eckert and Dr. John W. Mauchly in 1946 (p60) invented it. Some of them were tools manipulated by governments and for governments, which means that those data were strictly kept, analyzed, and used by minorities.

Because of their complex structures, more than one person or a number of people were needed to operate them. Besides the result was slow. Nowadays, more sophisticated computers or network systems, that have done more than the average, were designed to replace the mega ones. They produce more effective work, require one person or less than a number of people to monitor them, and they result in a short time comparing to the mega ones.

With the echo of the IBM Company a few decades ago, personal computer has gained the market trust and fed the desire for everyone to buy his/her own PC. Computers, since then, have become more familiar. There, they are everywhere in the stores, in the schools, and in the libraries exhibited for a demo or a more suited work.

City workers, some private institution workers, and a large number of students have had the benefit to learn more and achieve some goals on their own. Other than a house, a PC has also become a dream for every family or for every individual who wants to become a computer literate.

The application of the Internet and word processor has aspired everyone to look forward to such computer taste. "The demand for small computers in business and for scientific applications was so great that several companies manufactured only small computers (Larry and Nancy Long p67)."

Beyond microcomputers have lifted the market and made more appropriate the usage of computers. People who conduct a line of businesses such as Company CEO and consultant managers carry with them their lop top everywhere so that they can have all information desired available at a finger tip.

Today due to the evolution of computers, a person can relate to every part of the world and process data information. There is no frontier, no barrier what so ever for a person to connect with the exterior world and send or unload data. A portable computer can be used in cars running from one point to another, in planes, and in the oceans or under water.

Indeed, the evolution of computers has changed the patterns and the ways people used to live. A computer, today, is an objective machine behind every scene. Its contribution is huge and forfeits the need of every counter at each corner.

More importantly we are living the computer era. Soon or later you will have to know how to operate a computer to connect, communicate, and have more success in your business.

Do you know how to operate a computer??? Don't be surprised today in this actual age of computer I talk to people who have a degree from college that do not want to operate a computer. We do not want to judge anybody. We would like for you to only understand there are reasons for you to use a computer:

- When looking for resources

- When doing search queries

- When doing Projects or Assignments

- When implementing a business idea

- When managing time

Now that you learn the importances of having a computer make the effort to buy one and work on your project.

When you have the computer, note that you also make the decision to open the door to everything into your home. If you have a family takes the necessary precaution to prevent your children from viewing sites that are not educative for them.

Also remember you need to take necessary precaution to protect your computer against viruses that may damage it. To operate a computer or electronic devices has become imperative for most of us.

Advanced Technology has brought everything to light for the humanity to connect and communicate easily. You can now operate a system or your business from your car or your home.

If you are still behind, you need to start today. Take the time to learn and operate an electronic device that you like.

We understand that you would not make it without your wallet in the city, but if you were in a crisis, the only thing that would save your time would be your cell phone. Gadgets and gizmos are very common tools that people use nowadays to entertain, conduct business and so on. Due to their WiFi abilities to easily use Ape and connect.

Electronic Devices

After the success of the Apollo 11 returned back to earth from to the moon tin July 24, 1969 with the lead pilot Neil Armstrong and his crew, we acknowledged that we have more power with the extension of the satellites power on earth, which increased our ability to benefit more from electronic devices that require satellite power. This result also gave birth to a leading path in communication, which represents today one of the primary necessity for parents, teens, investors, businesses, and so on.

With the satellite result that empower our way of communication, we function nowadays with more wireless devices such as Gadgets and Gizmos.

 Gadgets and Gizmos are a selection of electronic devices that are more effective with wireless future (WIFI) and more profitable to everyone's needs and investments. To mention you need a cell phone:

- To stay in contact with others

- Maintain you activities

Looking forward to change or upgrade the electronic devices for your business will always increase the effect of your services and profit your customers. Some business owners use games to capture more or particular customers and make great profit.

Games have been always a satisfaction that drives our desires with passion to finish or get to the end with a winning score that lights our enjoyments.

Are you a winner?

If you are a winner you know the feelings, the enthusiasm and the confidence that purge your emotion.

It is not to forget a good game increases your

- Passion

- Ability to endure

- Confidence level

- And improves skills and techniques

You can easily find a game that you like, take time to learn it, and play it well so that you can be a winner. If you like the idea pick your choice.

Without any discretion as a business owner we encourage you to take the step to protect your identity. Often times we preoccupy ourselves with business transactions and totally forget how easy intentional outsiders can invade our privacy and use our frame our network to pickup our files.

Our special links:

Www.NewAvenue.US

Www.NewAvenue2020.com

http://www.earth24.me

Www.MoneyMaking.com

Identity Protection

Have you been taking the necessary steps to protect your identity? Today with the success of advanced technology everything is exposed. Your number or identity can be easily traced and used by unspecified trends to process transactions or complete other procedures under your names.

You truly do not want to be a candidate for something that is going to cost more to repair or affect the life of your business. Although we heard as much of that related news, we still think we have time or things are not going to happen to us.

Protect yourself and your family by keeping track of your records. We think that in the business of making money you might have to take this idea into consideration.

- Be Cautious about the way you handle your business transactions or the purchases you have done with credit cards.

- Do not let your personal information expose to others.

- Do not give others access to your personal information unless you know the reason.

When you are doing transactions remember to gather items and info before you leave the place. Be aware of the things that may occur and record your activities to prevent irregularities and protect yourself.

Take control of your situation. If you don't know what your situation looks like it is important to ask for help and research the resources to fix it. You do not explain your stories to the people who cannot help you. If you are in crisis look for that particular service that can offer solutions that relate to your problems.

Keep in mind that when you leave your information everywhere, you leave the opportunity to others to use your personal information or research the privileges that belong to you to their advantages. We would like for you to understand what we mean by having privileges. For instance, you have the privilege to drive because you have been a safe driver. However, if you were caught driving under the influence of alcohol or DUI your privilege would be taken away from you.

This is not a game it is true. Identity theft has become very common during the last decade. People have complained about their information stolen after using their credit cards, Internet, and so on.

Take the steps to protect yourself and make the right decision for yourself, your family, and your business. You may have to learn how to use a camera to collect evidence in case of occurrences.

Taking pictures to seal your records or knowing how to use a camera is a great idea when doing the moneymaking process. You can collect pictures for your business and take pictures to increase your portfolio impression or empower your presentation.

No need to be a professional. You can learn the basic skills to take simple pictures or use it for other purposes of your choice to make money.

Photography is one of the oldest applications that people still use today to keep the memory of their precious moments intact. If you had the idea to take pictures of your family five years ago for fun or doing special occasions, you would be still feeling happy that you did. The pictures that you took in the past can always make you laugh or remember special love ones when looking at them.

Besides taking pictures are a great learning skills and you can also make money with online photography today. You can take pictures from everywhere and make profit of them. People who have a passion for this do it on the street, on the beach, in the park and so on. You do not need to be a professional photographer to take pictures. You can walk to every alley or scenery and do like the professionals.

Carry your digital camera with you to the party, to your son football game, or any other event to explore sceneries. You can post them online, on your social network, and even participate in an art gallery. To learn more check the provided links:

Without standing, People use communication to establish relationship because they are seeking to connect with others. As we often observed, entrepreneurs travel to conduct business and establish relationship with allies. Have you ever taken some time to travel, to meet new people, visit family and friends, or just for fun to learn about other cultures, people interests, and trades. If you get to understand the three main questions that drive everybody's passion, you can best apply them when you explore other people ways of life.

I observed a child once in the plane asking his mother why, why, and why. I thought that child was ready to learn and experience a new adventure. You have the opportunity to explore how people live through their tradition when they commute and express themselves. Traveling is leaving to experience a great adventure that will stay with you for years. When you buy your ticket for that business trip, you will surely benefit from it.

If you understand the child curiosity you would admit that it is very important to ask questions or seek help when you do not comprehend the application you are working with. When you have the ability to defy or correct what stops you from going further, you will be surprised to see how confident you will be in the accomplishment of your work.

Make the plan to leave with your partner and use our resources. Take your love ones to an adventure. You can get an Airfare for a Disney world vacation or your tickets for a Cruise.

Our special links:

Www.NewAvenue.US

Www.NewAvenue2020.com

http://www.earth24.me

8 CONNECTION

In the old days people had friends, businesses, and made connections with people in their environments. They did not pay too much attention to group capacity.

People did not value much of connection since they used to apply traditional ways to communicate, connect, and conduct business with others. They could only benefit the specified services provided from telephone and television companies.

They had limited connections since they did not have the possibilities to develop strategies to reaching out large numbers. They had small groups and businesses that only served one community or two. Ways of communication were distant and took several days to a month for delivery.

Eventually, the improvements of computers and cell phones during the last decade have made it possible for people to develop strategies and connect to do business. People seek to connect more with others to share their interests and to increase their groups, association, or organizations' capacity. They have now the possibilities to connect within seconds through text messages, emails, and so on with a slight touch of the mouse.

The prominence of these tools facilitates the establishment for group discussion, conferences, and so on. They also provide strategies to implement applications and connect more effectively with others. Connection indeed that used to favor socializing in a more meticulous manner has become one of the first particular steps in business.

To illustrate, the existence of close circle, group, scholars, and your best friends are my friends were the legitimate ways to socialize and meet new friends. However, with the application of the tools we can now more diligently verify our participation and increase the capacity for members. Having the ability to connect helps to understand the importance of:

- Sharing information

- Identify interests

- Processing data

Most of us often do not know how to share information or not having the ability to connect with friends and others. We live in quarters and some of us only connect with friends and family members. We are preoccupied with our "to do task" and not even paying attention to others in our circle. We do not take part to activities other than our duties and go back home to sleep at the end of the day.

We are not informed about the upcoming or informed others about what we are able to share with them. We close our perimeters so that others do not know much of our deployed strategies. We live in the monotone of our days and only capture what comes our way instead of going after it and make it happen. The moneymaking process comes with requirements that will aspire others to engage in a particular activity in order to connect with others.

Not too much is required to connect and share, but at least one will have to use the tools to connect more with others. As we stated previously "being able to connect will increase our capacity to do business." If one were to make the effort to meet the requirement for data processing, he/she would have less to deal with at the end of the day.

When doing business it is very important to connect and identify others who share your interests for partnership, offering products, and demands. There are facts that reveal it is not always easy to find a partner to run a business. Partnership is an accord and engagement taken by two or more people who have the same interests to build an organization. When they do not have the same interests, they will become enemies and one in some way will destroy the other.

Connection in this manner has to be done in a more attentive and careful manner. Partners are not to jeopardize the structure of their business, which may impair their production and cause them to lose their investments. In business the main goal may be drawn for profit or company eligibility to offer services under the directive of state government. Whichever way might be a common accord is signed to validate partnership.

Partnership is the resolution to an organization ordered to provide services to communities, countries, and so on. A partnership helps the business to maintain a standard and meet the need of clients or customers. The partnership is to compensate to meet the need of the command that pertains to customer referral and business connection.

Customer referral and business connection are two factors that keep a business on the traffic map.

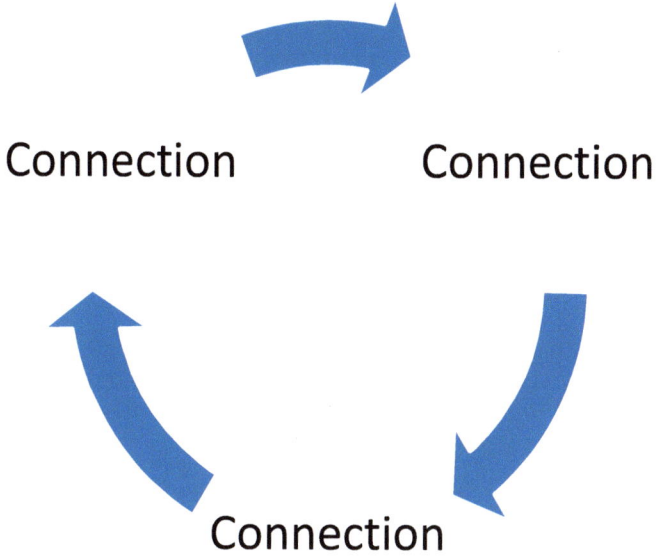

Connection

Connection

Connection

9 TOOLS & TREND

A child is not obligated to work to make a living, to fix to improve an element, or trade because parents or the people in charge are there to think for them, to fulfill their desires, and their needs. They do not have to fight or question the future. For a child having a job is an option. The only tool a child has to work with is education.

Often times children who do not have parents or people to provide for them struggle through their teenage years to find a job to support themselves or a tool to work with and make a living. At an early stage in life they seek to identify themselves and tend to rime with older friends since they did not have the opportunity to complete their childhood tasks.

Instead they learn to fix and implement their plans at a younger age since they have to respond to their responsibilities and face their reality.

In the moneymaking process you need at least to having a tool to work with in order to identify and represent your segments. There are various tools for everyone to choose from to make a living. From reading to science, technology, and so on, one will always find an element of interest to learn a skill.

A tool is what going to relate you to a particular trend. A tool will give you the ability to develop your skills, to experience and develop new applications, to earn, and contribute to the needs of your community. It is very important for everyone to understand the importance of making that choice. Without it you wouldn't have much to defy yourself or offer your service to others.

Our ancestors who did not have the opportunity to learn a skill had to decide to adopt a routine just to make a living. They had done a routine for years and did not have any profound knowledge of it. It is obvious that they used their routine as tools to present their services.

The most important part of it is that having a tool also requires to having the knowledge to manage it. A tool is not only what identifies you to others but it is also your talent to manifest and market yourself.

Many of us have difficulties to find a tool to work with due to lacking of resources, hardship, or not being able to select the right one. For instance, when I went to college, some of the students were undecided about what subject they wanted to major in. So they changed a few times until they felt comfortable to learn the skills of that particular field. Tools are relatively selected to meet the individual interest because more can be explored and experienced in that manner.

Many do not choose the right tool due to financial situation and not having the satisfied requirements for programs assistance or scholarships. Consequently they have to do some preparation or choose something more appropriate to start with to fill in the gap.

Some others just do not have the resources to make the proper connection to find the tool that they want to use. Even though the resources are available online and at the respective centers, if the individual is not a computer savvy the research process alone can take time.

Finding the right tool to use can be easy at times, but it also requires some efforts on the user part to make the discovery. It might sound very ironic to realize that you have to learn to fix something to support your family and to fulfill your dreams.

If you are still confused about what you want to do, you can simply ask yourself.

- What tool can I use to plan my future?

- What can I fix to make a living?

Once you understand the concept of having a tool you will be very glad for making that forward step. Then it will be easier to keep the tool, change it, or even work with more tools.

The tendency to improve the knowledge and open the market to others is what really making a difference. For many years many of us did not quiet understand the importance of using a tool to make money. They even made the assumptions that the ones who use the tools were not professionals; however, when they open the surgeon room of operation they were confused.

To see it clearly the professional would neither making a difference nor feeling comfortable working with the potential clients without using a tool.

Due to those factors most of companies have relied on computers programming and operations to validate their work or implement their tools.

10 DATA PROCESSING

Processing data which means sending, receiving, and filling data has become more common, easier, and more reputable over years. Prior to the computer age, businesses used pencils, ink, and notebooks to report, collect, and keep records. It requires for someone to being organized and having profound computer skills to do that portion of the job.

Today having a basic knowledge of computer, a simple software installment or training is enough to help someone operate a business. Few decades ago some business owners did not care too much about keeping records of their customers' transactions; which has affected the growth of their businesses.

Sending and receiving data have been always an important element in business. Most owners neglected that portion before due to the time effort and the high pay to engage someone to do the job. Now it is highly recommended to process data and keep these records because businesses use these data to promote more than one application such as:

- To understand and improve the condition of the business

- To provide better services to customers

- To develop their media profile and folder

When keeping the records business owners have the ability to understand how their businesses are doing for the fiscal year and predict the outcomes for profit or deficit. Using the data received, owners can easily identify the matter and offer alternatives to manage the situation that impair the condition of the businesses.

Sending data help businesses to maintain their competition and increase their credibility with business associates and customers. Sending data is used to offer product to customers and process response to orders and other requirements.

With the assistance of advanced technology most businesses do well today in sending data to complete file documents. With one touch of the mouse one can email and fax to forward document.

When data have not been confirmed to be received or sent, there is an indication that one of the segments designed or responsible to secure the connection is impaired. Sometimes it can be just a matter of computer software used or the person in placed to complete the task. Many companies received a lot of customer service complaints only as a result of that simple matter.

Data processing gives to owners the ability and privilege to analyze the frequency of demands and offer better services to customers. With the exploration of advanced technology business owners are now understand the importance and the advantages of data processing. They use it to satisfy the demand and increase their businesses capacity.

Data processing also used to develop Medias that include any or various types of associations, organizations, or groups. Media folders are used to facilitate reaching out members and increase the level of capacity.

With the media acknowledgement that involves marketing most businesses do better with the application of data processing. With advanced technology most businesses have the ability to send and receive data within the window expected time.

Some companies received customer complaints due to data processing because the information fails to reach the other departments for following up.

When the data is not processed, received, or sent, there is an indication that the connections are impaired or the function is not well defined. Sometimes it might be just a matter with the failure of computer software or the person responsible to complete the task is not aware of the occurrence.

Data processing is the most common method used in businesses today because it offers ways to implement and develop resources, ability to identify tools that match the request or the matter, and ability to connect with others. We encourage verifying your data to understand your business performance.

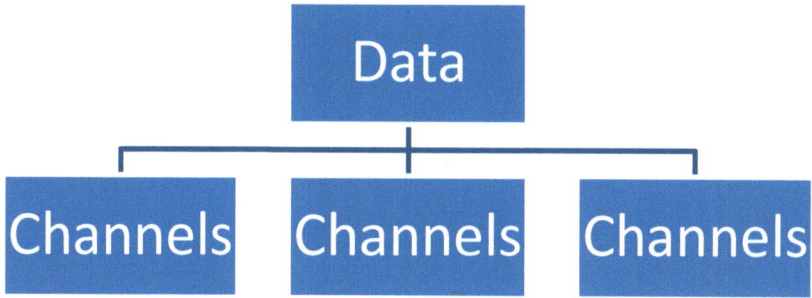

ABOUT THE AUTHOR

I, Garry Louis, was born on an Island, Haiti, a Caribbean country that still keeps his old traditions and values with its culture. My parents and my grandmother raised me. Between my father and my mother, I am the baby of a family of 7 children: three males and four females. My father had served my country as a Captain in the army, and my mother had been in the past a regular business entrepreneur before she retired.

I finished school in my country and went to work for the city as an inspector in education under the direction of the Department of Planification. There I learned a few things especially about cooperative organization, which was then one of the biggest enterprises in my country. My mother left my country and went to establish in Canada and Puerto Rico in the late 70's before moving to Miami to make room for the rest of the family. We followed her after exploring a few years in Canada.

I always have good relationship with my mother even though when she was away for a while to make a living. My brothers and sisters love me a lot, but we all different in some ways. I am layback and a very positive person. I am very goal oriented, and I have good determination to fulfill my dreams.

When I was a kid, I wanted to be an economist, an entrepreneur, and a musician like one of my older cousins. However, when I started to work in my country I fulfilled some line of positions as a bookkeeper and credit cooperator, and I did more than I was expected to do in that field.

I never get to be a musician because one of my older sisters didn't like the idea of me becoming a musician, playing festivals, or music in the bars. At that time musicians in my country were very productive and the effort to rank among them required a lot of practice.

I started in the past as an entrepreneur for a number of years, and I was doing well until L decided to leave my country due to the affect of political situation that drained the market. The country was in chaos; I lost a lot of money. Since then I have been trying to perceive things another way and apply new approaches to secure my investments.

For my career, I was supposed to pursue a two years study in Canada, but I decided to start again for a long shot in the U.S. Psychologically, I am very stable. I think that since I was a child I learned some principles that shape my personality as a person.

Even though when I was a kid I didn't know much about personality or who I was, I live up to see the reflection of my father, a man who served his country and died for the cause of others. In addition, somewhere down the line I believe I looked up to one of my uncles and two of my cousins as significant figures in my family and my role models.

To mention I have had some negative experiences. Things or situations that either hurt my feelings directly or indirectly and left me with bitter sorrow mood, or deep sadness.

One of the negatives experiences I had stays with me until today. When I was 16 year old I had two best females' friends: my girlfriend and her sister. Their parents were about to leave my country for the U.S.

After they departed from my country I was left alone without a best friend. We had good correspondence. I planned to visit them the following summer, but a terrible event had occurred and countered our time.

One night my girlfriend's sister was left alone at her house and got sick. When her father came back home from work he found her in a trouble state. She was gasping for breath fighting for her life. Her father rushed her to the hospital. She didn't make it. She passed away there. She was a very passionate, nice, and friendly person.

Her death left me with sadness for a long time every moment I thought of her. I could not admit that she was gone. After a number of years I have learned how to deal with that. Eventually, she will be always in my memory. She was a special friend. May she rest in peace!

I had another negative experience when I was 23 years of age. I primarily had good plan to get married at 25 years old and have a blessing family. I was working and making good money enough to support a family, but that old drama changed my dream and twisted my life and my plans around.

One night, my girlfriend called to tell me we could not be together anymore. I was her first boyfriend, and she was my only real girlfriend. After she told me that I didn't want to believe her because we had a long history together. We had been together for more than five years. We grew up together and participated in numerous activities together. She left me and could not really give me a reason. I was confused.

We had many good habits together. We used to go to the same church and sing together on many occasions. Her family (her dad, mom, and sisters) liked me a lot, and my family had a lot of admiration for her. Everybody knew we were together, and we seemed to be a perfect couple at that time.

I was suddenly become unhappy, and I did everything in my power to conquer her heart back. I kept trying for the following two years to convince her to get back together. When I could finally accept her decision, she came back and asked me to reconsider our relationship. My mother has always liked her and was on her side. Yet, I had fear to be left alone a second time for no reason. I told her no to resolve my case. But I was still lost.

Since I was ready to have a family, and my girlfriend dumped me, Freud's assumption would be I got fixated because I was too caring for my girlfriend. His theory about genital stage would perceive my case as an individual who had some neurotic conflict between my biological demands and the requirement of understanding from my girlfriend.

One of the worst experiences I got when I came in to the Miami area a few years ago was finding a job. I applied for job everywhere: Malls, Miami down town stores, schools, down town offices, etc. It was difficult for me to find a job in the first place.

After a couple of months I started a night shift job in a store working 12:00am to 8:00am (not in a good area). I didn't like the job or the schedule but I needed a start. The workplace was not safe, and the customers I got were very demanding, confronting, offensive, and dangerous.

Among those customers were thieves, criminals, buglers, etc. I went to work every night praying God to make it through because a few bad cases had been reported at that store during the previous years. I never said anything to my mother. I kept everything to myself.

One night I went to work as usual, and saw a car was cruising in the store parking lot every two hours. At exactly 4:00 am the car came back and stopped by at my transaction door. There were four men in the car. The driver wanted to buy a pack of cigarettes. By the time I was getting the cigarettes for him, another one got off the car, got in the store and put a gun in my right hear.

For a minute I experienced death right in front of me. But I was cool and said to the man take whatever you want in the store. With the gun in my head, the men madly said open the register. I opened the register and the man got all the money (a pity sum of $80) and he left with the others.

When they completely left the store parking lot I dialed 911. That phone call last about 20 minutes or more of interrogation. The officer asked me a list of questions to kill time. Next I called the store manager. She told me to close everything and she will be there. She arrived 10 minutes after and told me to go home.

I went home early that morning and said nothing to my mother. I was off the following day and felt a great relief. When it was time for me to get back to work my anxiety level increased. Then, I decided to tell my mother, and she told me to quit the job of course. That was one of the worst experiences I had, and I surely didn't want to experience the worst.

Nevertheless, there were times I knew some neutral events in my life. I saw them as things that were there to help me discover the good in me or in other people. I didn't get any result from those events most of the time; but they were to occur, and I was there to perform and learn.

A few years ago, I used to work in a store in Miami where I used to have a lot of customers and done a lot of transactions for the store. I used to work 4:00 pm to 12:00 am, and that particular time I would meet a lot of important people almost every day. One of my customers, a woman, was very nice.

One day, I decided to talk to her and ask her for some direction to find another job. She listened and told me to come to her office located in down town Miami. That morning I got there on time, well dressed, and asked to see her. The lady at the desk answered, "You want to see the Commissioner."

I had no idea that she was the highest figure in that office department. Her secretary took my name and had me waited. A few minutes after, the Commissioner greeted me into her office. We spoke for a minute; then she called her secretary, told her to give me an application, and had me applied for a position. I was well treated with a lot of respects. Unfortunately, I could not perform the job she gave me due to lacking of English skills.

I refused the offer and left a note for her saying I want to try something else. The very next time she saw me again, she said to me "you could do it." I explained to her I couldn't write English well, and that I needed more time to perform such tasks. That lady motivated me more to pursue my goals and reach my dreams. I consider that intervention to be neutral because the result I got from it was neither good nor bad, but still benefited me in some way.

A significant period of my life started with happiness and rewards earned from the effort I put in playing soccer for my team in my country. I was 21 year old, another best friend of mine, and the team members we bit up and won every single game we ever played.

Our big expectation was to make it through the final in order to get qualified for a national championship competition. The team was doing excellently well, and people from every corner of my country had great admiration for the players.

The team won the championship and got qualified as we were expected, but the national championship never took place. The country was in chaos at that time, and political news was the only broadcasting news 24/7. Consequently, the team reputation disappeared, and their social and economic status changed due to lack of practice and political obstacles.

After a few years most of the players and I decided to leave the country and explore life somewhere else. Unfortunately, we went different locations and never got to play together again. As a result of the effort we put in to get us somewhere did not do any good or bad. The team reached the level as expected, fulfilled the hope, and never got to become bigger. The players went to different places; they got older and live the memories until today.

I have learned to solve or have hands on issues that needed to be addressed. I felt guilty because I blamed myself for I wasn't focused enough to prepare another plan for the team.

Among all the positive things I registered in my life, these are the most recent significant ones I can recall. They are in fact very challenging, and I do appreciate that I have been fortunate to overcome obstacles and being able to put pieces together to solve the puzzle.

Adaptation is one of the positive factors that I experienced. When I finally resided in Miami, life was not easy for me. I had to learn almost about everything to regain my independency, such as language, locations, streets, and bus terminals from one point to another.

I learned every English word I could to keep up my pace and to communicate better with people. I studied hard for days and most likely nights to overcome my weakness. After a few months I could do a lot of things by myself. I could go places and applying for jobs. I got my driver license and started to drive.

That was a good feeling: a feeling of being independent and responsible. I kept my things organized and learned all the necessary skills to prevent myself from having trouble or falling into bizarre situations that I didn't have no knowledge about. I sought information that I needed to guide myself into the system. I got a job and went back to school at the same time.

I was trapped among tight schedules, unexpected plans, and tiny budgets, but I got hope and that was enough to keep me going and reassuring myself. I got married and got divorced. However, my independency had given me the strength that I needed to overcome my situation and keep my lifestyle. I have a daughter.

I learned the culture to understand values and be able to comprehend things around me in the milieu. I have met a lot of people since then, and I have done my best to have good relationships with them.

Another positive thing that I before experienced in my life was about to happen again when I got here. I was working for a company that contracted transactions with an airline at Miami airport International once.

My work was to get the cargo on time and drive the airline crew mostly pilots safely to their planes. I used to do my work very well and often got rewarded from the clients. The manager liked my work and my way of doing things continuously.

My English with a heavy accent wasn't great, yet my effort as a hard worker and my relationship with the coworkers classified me as a good team worker. The manager had observed my work and asked me if I wanted to be part of another team for a new contract. I said yes and suddenly I had another job.

The new job contract didn't have a schedule. Six of us were chosen within the company to carry the contract, and we were on call if we were not on the airport field. The tasks were not difficult since we were doing the same thing but extra work with another airline.

The manager would call us sometimes at 1, 2, or 3 am including dayshift an hour prior to the plane arrival. The schedule was difficult to manage, but the money was good. I worked the contract for three months and went to work for another company.

I have always looked at those steps like I was being promoted. When I was in my country I got promoted once, and I know how that feels. Promotion creates another line for me in my life that I always strive for.

When I was younger I used to have one prayer: to finish with school and be on my own. Then I finished school in my country; I enjoyed a few years and went right back into schooling. Engaging myself in school in the U.S. was one of the most difficult decisions I had to make to shape my reality.

When I left my country I had the option to continue with a tow years scholarship in Canada or France since I speak French or go for a long term in the U.S. starting with learning English. Thus, I focused on the tough choice to gain more in return.

I am glad I can say that going back to school is one of the most counted positive experiences I have.

I came from a long way to re-identify myself in a new community and even a New World. I have been putting a lot of years into that bag to get to this point. Today I am bilingual and sometimes trilingual. I have talked to people from different tribes and countries. I said that because I talk Creole to people from other country and French to my oldest friends.

In addition, as a transferred student from Miami Dade Community College, I took the path to Florida A & M University where I earned a master's degree that truly encouraged me to achieve my goals and pursue my field of study. I have known some ups and downs, but it worth it to see the result I am getting out of this.

In my earlier years in Miami, when I started to go back to school, the length of my achievement time was very long. I used to want to jump or take a short cut to reach my goals, but realistically there were none available. My struggle was tensed, but I was determined to discover another side of reality.

Today I am glad that I didn't quit when looking back to those years. I managed to maintain in order to win a good fight.

Five years from now I will be in the real world as a professional working with a lot of clients. I will guide my clients and provide them necessary tools to help them discover their world. I will have the certitude that my help will have potential effect in others' lives.

This Biography is reviewed to reflect my past, my backgrounds, and give credit to one of my teachers at Florida A & M University: Dr. Allan Bellups

Index

MoneyMaking

MoneyMaking is a 1-2-3-step process that requires no profound knowledge but discipline

MoneyMaking Process

MoneyMaking Process is a simple method that describes a 1/3 principle to help individuals to earn a living and also teach them how to invest to earn great returns at the end of the investment term.

Business

A business is a legitimate way to create a signature for yourself. It gives a unique impression to your friends, family, society you are a part of, and even expose your performance to the world you live in.

Having a Business

Having a business is to offer a service and/or product that meet the requirement to satisfy the need of a community that might be local or international.

Marketing

Marketing is one of the major practices to promote a business.

Advertisement

Advertisement is a method to communicate your service and/or product to others through various types of applications and channels.

Flyer

Flyer is a simple application and effective way to reach out targeted customers.

Ad/Online Ad

Ad is a service or product short description of use as an application displays on search engines to capture potential customers.

Presentation

A presentation can be used as an advertisement form or application to defy a business and its service or product.

Media

Media is one of the leading forms of service and/or product advertisement through channels that companies use to reach out a great number of customers/clients in no time.

Media Channels

Media Channels are magazines, newspaper, radio & TV broadcasts, and 300 plus online channels.

Event

Event has become a form of advertisement that companies recently use to capture their fans, potential customers, and sell their products.

Blogging

Blogging is one of the common forms of advertisement and application tool that individuals, businesses, professionals use today to share their idea, experiences, and market their products.

Tool

A tool is an object used to fix broken elements.

Using a Tool

Using a tool requires to having the knowledge to manage it. Your tool is your talent to manifest and market yourself.

1/3 Principle

1/3 Principle is a concept designed to help business owners and entrepreneurs to structure their business plans and increase their profit margins.

Announcement

In the following editions we will discuss more about business tools, marketing tools, business connection, tool & trend, investment, product displayed, 1/3 Principle, and data processing. The moneymaking concept will provide for you the strategies to make money in no time.

Bio References

Corey, G. (2001). Theory and practice of counseling and psychotherapy. (6th Ed.).

Susan C. Cloninger (2000). Theories of personality: Understanding persons. (3rd Ed.). Upper Saddle River, New Jersey. Prentice Hall

Sharf, R. S. (2002). Applying career development theory to counseling. (3rd. Ed.).

Graph References:
www.shutterstock.com
www.google.com
Google Graph Chart
www.dreamstime.com

AUTHOR: Garry Louis PhD. In Health Management & Policy

ISBN-13: 978-0615917184 (NewAvenue)

www.ingramcontent.com/pod-product-compliance
Lightning Source LLC
Chambersburg PA
CBHW041312210326
41599CB00003B/84